ME TOO!®
B O O K S

THE GREAT SHAKE-UP

MIRACLES IN PHILIPPI

By Marilyn Lashbrook

Illustrated by Chris Sharp

RAINBOW
STUDIES
INTERNATIONAL

El Reno, Oklahoma

Creating Colorful Treasures™

ME TOO! ® Books are designed to help you share the joy of reading with children. They provide a new and fun way to improve a child's reading skills — by practice and example. At the same time, you are teaching your child valuable Bible truths.

Why do bad things sometimes happen to people who obey God? THE GREAT SHAKE-UP will help children understand God's purpose in allowing problems. At the same time, they will hear the Gospel message and see how one family responded joyfully. This story will present you with an opportunity to discuss with children the importance of accepting Jesus as Savior, the power a believer has to live a new kind of life, and the responsibility each believer has to praise God and share his or her faith.

Reading is the key to successful education. Obeying the principles of God's Word opens the door to a successful life. **ME TOO!**® Books encourage your children in both!

Bold type: Child reads.
Regular type: Adult reads.

 Wait for child to respond.

 Talk about it!

Library of Congress Catalog Card Number: 90-63768
ISBN 0-933657-84-6

Copyright © 1991 and 1998 by Rainbow Studies, Inc.
All rights reserved. Printed in Mexico.

Art direction and design by
Chris Schechner Graphic Design.

1 2 3 4 5 6 7 8 9 — 02 01 00 99
Rainbow Studies International, El Reno, OK 73036, U.S.A.

THE GREAT SHAKE-UP

MIRACLES IN PHILIPPI

Taken from Acts 16

Paul and Silas hurried along the road to a place of prayer outside Philippi. They came to this city to share God's Good News with everyone they met. A woman named Lydia and others who believed in Jesus were going to the prayer meeting with Paul and Silas.

Suddenly a slave girl started yelling. She followed the little group of believers, shouting all the way.

The girl was a fortune teller. She was owned by men who charged people to hear their fortunes. The men were getting very rich.

But the slave girl was not happy. She had an evil spirit inside of her. She did not want to do things she did. But she could not stop.

The slave girl followed Paul and Silas for days. Finally, Paul was so upset, he said to the spirit, "In the name of Jesus Christ I command you to come out of her!"

Instantly, the spirit came out. God's power changed the girl's life in less time than it takes to sneeze. The girl would never tell fortunes again.

She was glad to be free. At last, she could make her own choices.

But her owners were very angry. They could not use her to make money anymore. They did not care about the girl. They only cared about making money.

The owners grabbed Paul and Silas and dragged them through the hot, dusty streets. Curious people followed to see what would happen. When they reached the city leaders, Paul and Silas found themselves surrounded by a big, noisy crowd.

Why was this happening? Paul and Silas were not criminals! They were missionaries. Why do you think bad things sometimes happen to people who love God? ⬣

"These men are shaking up our whole city!" the people said. "They are teaching others to break Roman laws."

"Throw them in jail," said the ruler. "Guard them carefully."

The jailor knew he would be in big trouble if Paul and Silas escaped. So he took them to an inner cell. He fastened their feet in stocks and chained their arms. "Bang!" The door slammed shut and locked.

This was a fine place for Christians to be. It was downright embarassing. But Paul and Silas had nothing to feel guilty about. They were not in jail for doing something wrong. And they had nothing to worry about. God knew exactly where they were, and He had a plan for them.

It took time for the men's eyes to adjust to the darkness in the jail cell. And they didn't like what they saw.

The jail cells were dirty

and smelly

and soggy

and buggy.

Some of the prisoners were sick. All of them were lonely. Some deserved to be in jail, but it still made Paul and Silas sad to see men in such a state.

God loves all people - whether they are a little bit bad or a whole lot bad. Jesus died for these men too.

There was no way for Paul and Silas to get comfortable. No matter how much they wiggled and squirmed, they were stuck in the same position. Their legs ached and their backs grew stiff.

The two men couldn't sleep, but they could pray! God is always awake and listening. He heard their prayer. Soon they would see His answer.

They could sing, too. It was late at night, so they sang softly. But singing about Jesus cheered them up.

The more they sang, the better they felt. And the better they felt, the louder they sang. Before they knew it, they forgot all about their problems. They sang joyfully at the top of their lungs. Do you ever sing when you feel sad? How does it make you feel? ⬢

The other men in the jail listened. The songs about God's love made them feel better too.

Even the guard could tell there was something different about Paul and Silas. They were so determined to obey God. They were so sure God would take care of them.

Soon a peaceful feeling came over the jailor, and he fell sound asleep.

At midnight there was an earthquake, but it wasn't an ordinary one, for God caused all of the prison doors to fly open. And all of the chains broke and fell from the prisoners arms. This was a miracle - an answer to prayer!

Even though there was nothing holding them, the prisoners did not run away. Every one of them stayed in his prison cell.

When the jailor woke up and saw the doors standing open, he was really shook up! The punishment for allowing prisoners to escape was a slow and painful death. The jailor decided he would rather die quickly.

"Stop!" Paul shouted. "We are all here!"

The guard was amazed…and very relieved. He came trembling to their cell and fell on his knees before Paul and Silas. "Sirs," the jailor blurted out, "What must I do to be saved?"

"Believe." Paul answered. "Believe on the Lord Jesus Christ and you will be saved. You and your whole family."

The man did want his family to hear about Jesus. "Please come," he said. "Come tell my family how to be saved."

So Paul and Silas told the jailor's loved ones that Jesus died to pay for all their sins. "Jesus was buried," they said, "And He came back to life three days later!"

The jailor's whole family believed in the Lord Jesus to forgive their sins. God gave them new life.

Then the jailor took Paul and Silas to the river to wash the sores where they were beaten. While they were there, Paul and Silas baptized the jailor and his family.

Afterwards they went back to the house for something to eat. The whole family was filled with joy because they believed in God now. It was the best night of their lives.

At last their guilt and fear was gone. They had a reason to live. They felt real peace for the first time in their lives.

And best of all, they would be together forever in Heaven with God. Now there was light and laughter and love in their home.

Soon, the sun would crawl over the horizon. The jailor had to sneak his prisoners back to their cells while it was still dark.

Paul and Silas did not mind. Now they knew why God let them go to jail.

It wasn't just the people in church who needed to hear about Jesus. God's love was for everyone.

Later that day, the city leaders brought Paul and Silas out of jail. "Now stop talking about God," the leaders warned. "and leave our city today!"

Then Paul and Silas walked away from the city of Philippi. But they did not stop praying. And they did not stop telling people about Jesus.

Everywhere they went, people listened and their hearts were shaken up. People believed and their lives were changed. Soon the whole world was talking about Jesus, the wonderful Son of God. 💜💛

ME TOO!®
B O O K S

Ages 2-7

SOMEONE TO LOVE THE STORY OF CREATION	**NO TREE FOR CHRISTMAS** THE STORY OF JESUS' BIRTH
TWO BY TWO THE STORY OF NOAH'S FAITH	**NOW I SEE** THE STORY OF THE MAN BORN BLIND
I DON'T WANT TO THE STORY OF JONAH	**DON'T ROCK THE BOAT** THE STORY OF THE MIRACULOUS CATCH
I MAY BE LITTLE THE STORY OF DAVID'S GROWTH	**OUT ON A LIMB** THE STORY OF ZACCHAEUS
I'LL PRAY ANYWAY THE STORY OF DANIEL	**SOWING AND GROWING** THE PARABLE OF THE SOWER AND THE SOILS
WHO NEEDS A BOAT? THE STORY OF MOSES	**DON'T STOP. . . FILL EVERY POT** THE STORY OF THE WIDOW'S OIL
GET LOST, LITTLE BROTHER THE STORY OF JOSEPH	**GOOD, BETTER, BEST** THE STORY OF MARY AND MARTHA
THE WALL THAT DID NOT FALL THE STORY OF RAHAB'S FAITH	**GOD'S HAPPY HELPERS** THE STORY OF TABITHA AND FRIENDS

Ages 5-10

IT'S NOT MY FAULT MAN'S BIG MISTAKE	**NOTHING TO FEAR** JESUS WALKS ON WATER	**NOBODY KNEW BUT GOD** MIRIAM AND BABY MOSES
GOD, PLEASE SEND FIRE ELIJAH AND THE PROPHETS OF BAAL	**THE BEST DAY EVER** THE STORY OF JESUS	**MORE THAN BEAUTIFUL** THE STORY OF ESTHER
TOO BAD, AHAB NABOTH'S VINEYARD	**THE GREAT SHAKE-UP** MIRACLES IN PHILIPPI	**FAITH TO FIGHT** THE STORY OF CALEB
THE WEAK STRONGMAN SAMSON	**TWO LADS AND A DAD** THE PRODIGAL SON	**BIG ENEMY, BIGGER GOD** THE STORY OF GIDEON

WE SEE!™
V I D E O S

VIDEOS FOR TODAY'S CHRISTIAN FAMILY.
*51 animated Bible stories from the Old Testament ("In the Beginning" Series) and
New Testament ("A Kingdom without Frontiers" Series) will provide your children
with a solid cornerstone of spiritual support.*

Available at your local bookstore or from:
Rainbow Studies International • P.O. Box 759 • El Reno, Oklahoma 73036
1-800-242-5348

RSI
Creating Colorful Treasure.